Homeland Security and Counterterrorism Careers

Secret Service Agent

and Careers in Federal Protection

Homeland Security and

Counterterrorism Careers

Air Marshal
and Careers in Transportation Security
ISBN: 0-7660-2647-7

Border Patrol Agent
and Careers in Border Protection
ISBN: 0-7660-2646-9

Operations Officer
and Careers in the CIA
ISBN: 0-7660-2649-3

Search and Rescue Specialist
and Careers in FEMA
ISBN: 0-7660-2650-7

Secret Service Agent
and Careers in Federal Protection
ISBN: 0-7660-2651-5

Special Agent
and Careers in the FBI
ISBN: 0-7660-2648-5

Homeland Security and Counterterrorism Careers

Secret Service Agent

and Careers in Federal Protection

by Gerry Souter

Enslow Publishers, Inc.
40 Industrial Road
Box 398
Berkeley Heights, NJ 07922
USA
http://www.enslow.com

Library of Congress Cataloging-in-Publication Data

Souter, Gerry.
Secret service agent and careers in federal protection / Gerry Souter.
p. cm. — (Homeland security and counterterrorism careers)
Includes bibliographical references and index.
ISBN: 0-7660-2651-5
1. United States. Dept. of Homeland Security—Vocational guidance—Juvenile literature. 2. United States. Dept. of Homeland Security—Officials and employees—Juvenile literature. 3.Terrorism—United States—Prevention—Juvenile literature. 4. National security—United States—Juvenile literature. 5. Civil defense—United States—Juvenile literature. I. Title.
HV6432.4.S693 2006
363.28'302373—dc22

2006025259

Printed in the United States of America

10 9 8 7 6 5 4 3 2 1

To Our Readers:
We have done our best to make sure all Internet Addresses in this book were active and appropriate when we went to press. However, the author and the publisher have no control over and assume no liability for the material available on those Internet sites or on other Web sites they may link to. Any comments or suggestions can be sent by e-mail to comments@enslow.com or to the address on the back cover.

Photo Credits: Associated Press, AP, pp. 5, 14–15, 16, 23, 33, 35, 36, 38, 51, 106; 2006 by Colt Defense LLC, used with permission, all rights reserved, p. 61; Corbis/Ramin Talaie, p. 32; FEMA, pp. 5, 7, 12, 30, 70, 103, 116, 118, 121, 123, 125, 126, 128; Getty Images, pp. 6, 19, 21, 34, 44, 47, 49, 56, 86, 97, 108; Getty Images/AFP, pp. 5, 8, 11, 42, 43, 68–69, 83, 109, 111; Getty Images/Time Life Pictures, p. 95; Library of Congress, pp. 17, 20, 26, 27; U.S. Department of Defense, pp. 77, 117, 119; U.S. Immigration and Customs Enforcement, pp. 3, 5, 54, 55, 65, 73, 81, 85, 87, 99, 120, 122, 124, 127.

Cover Photo: Corbis/Darryl Bush/San Francisco Chronicle, Corbis/Royalty-Free (background)

Contents

Secret Service agents protect President George W. Bush's motorcade during the 55th Presidential Inaugural Parade on January 20, 2005.

Chapter 1

Two Agencies: Protecting Leaders and the People They Serve

The United States Secret Service had to take a chance. President George W. Bush was about to take a tour of New Orleans, Louisiana. It was late summer in 2005. Hurricane Katrina had just struck the city. Normally, a bubble of protection surrounds the president when he leaves the White House. Agents drive a parade of SUVs in the president's motorcade. The president travels in an extra-heavy bomb-proof and bulletproof car. Counterterrorism squads watch everything around the motorcade.

In New Orleans that day, the protective bubble had to be lifted. There was no time for advance planning. Streets were flooded. None of the usual precautions

Counter-sniper units include a rifleman and a spotter. These teams scan the area surrounding the president with eagle eyes.

were possible. A few rooftop counter-sniper units were available. These two-person teams include a rifleman and a spotter. Together they scan the streets for hidden attackers who may target the president or other people. On a normal presidential visit, buildings along the streets where Bush travels are cleared of people. That job was unnecessary. The hurricane and flooding had already emptied the heart of the city.

What precautions were possible? First, almost no planes were allowed to fly over a sixty-mile area around the city. Only planes under control of the Federal

The hurricane and flooding had already emptied the heart of the city.

Aviation Administration could fly through that zone. It was through this area that *Marine One,* the president's helicopter, traveled.

With a jet whine and the thudding beat of its rotor blades, *Marine One* landed on the deck of the USS *Iwo Jima*. This assault ship was the floating headquarters for the Katrina flood-relief mission docked on the Mississippi River. Secret Service agents lined the railings as the president went below deck for a briefing. President Bush spent the night aboard the *Iwo Jima*. The next morning, guarded by more agents, President Bush boarded one of four specially equipped

U.S. Army trucks. He continued on his tour through the city.

The president and his party stood in an open truck bed. Flood water, greenish muck, and debris sucked at the truck's tires. The passengers had to stoop down to avoid dangling power wires. A news reporter in another truck watched the president as the vehicles churned through mud-choked streets. He remarked to his fellow reporters that he had never seen a president riding under open sky, rather than in a limousine or armored vehicle. The reporter had not been alive the last time a president had ridden publicly in an open car—President John F. Kennedy on the day of his assassination, November 22, 1963.[1]

Surrounding the president were Secret Service agents charged with protecting him. The president was exposed. The situation was dangerous. But at the end of the day, *Marine One* lifted off from the *Iwo Jima* with the president safely aboard. The president continued on to view more of the storm's destruction. The agents moved to the next location where they would be needed. The Secret Service never stopped its normal operations. It only changed to fit the special situation of Hurricane Katrina.

Not far away, another group of federal officers was providing help after the hurricane. Federal Protective Service (FPS) officers had driven sixteen hours from Chicago to Baton Rouge, Louisiana. They joined officers from other cities at the relief headquarters. Then they made their way into New Orleans.

Hurricane Katrina flooded New Orleans so completely that it was impossible to provide President Bush with normal protection during his visit.

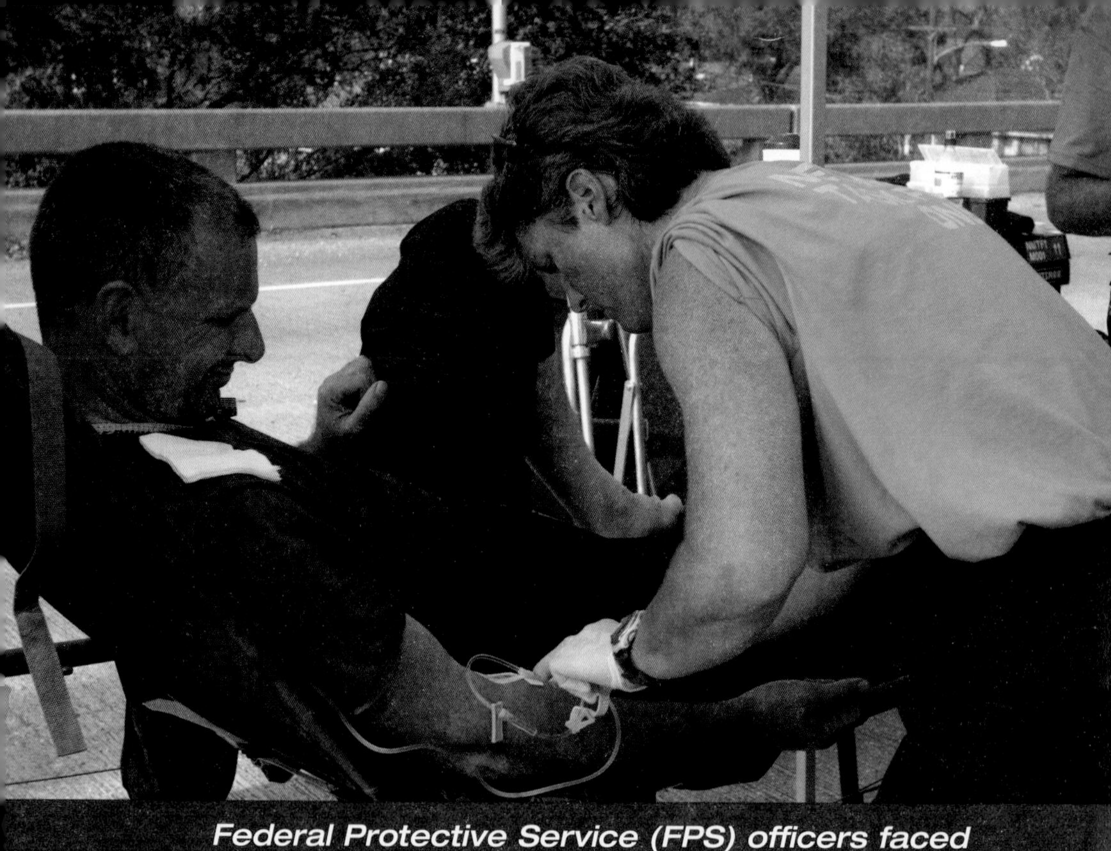

Federal Protective Service (FPS) officers faced many challenges in the aftermath of Katrina. A FPS team member receives medical treatment from a Federal Emergency Management Agency worker.

During the early days of the tragedy, police were spread thin. Thousands of people were crowded into the Louisiana Superdome. Water, wind, and destruction had forced them out of their homes. A thousand National Guard troops protected the outside of the dome. Inside, thirty-five Disaster Medical Assistance Team volunteers worked hard to relieve some of the suffering. These volunteers relied on only sixteen FPS officers for their security. People in the Superdome were frustrated, angry, and afraid.

The FPS officers worked as police to protect people and property. It was a difficult job, both physically and emotionally.

The FPS officers worked as police to protect people and property. They also did many other important jobs. They helped families find relief services. They comforted lost children. They reunited family members. In short, they did what they could to help other Americans. It was a difficult job, both physically and emotionally.

Meanwhile, at other points in New Orleans, gunshots rang out in deserted streets. An FPS team backed up state police in a shootout on a bridge across the Mississippi River. The officials were trying to stop gangs. They had taken over whole neighborhoods and were looting and vandalizing them.

In one U.S. city devastated by a shocking natural disaster, two federal protection agencies had come together. Both performed their jobs well in service to the American people.

Hurricane Katrina Challenges Law Enforcement

By Friday, August 26, 2005, officials in New Orleans knew a hurricane would strike their area. By August 28, evacuation of the city had begun. Thirty thousand people hurried into the Superdome sports stadium. About thirty-six hours' worth of food and supplies were available. The next day, the storm crashed into the city. The concrete and steel levees (walls) that held back Lake Pontchartrain and the Mississippi River began to crumble. Pumps failed. Water rushed through the lower parts of the city. Neighborhoods were cut off from electric power, sewer sanitation, food, fresh water, and police protection.

On August 29, law enforcement began arriving to support the local and state police. Immigration and Customs Enforcement (ICE) sent about 725 law enforcement and support personnel from around the country to the Gulf Coast.[2] There were more than four hundred special agents from ICE's Office of Investigations, two hundred officers from the Federal Protective Service, and one hundred officers from Detention and Removal Operations. There were also eight Special Response Teams of highly trained armed personnel (right).[3]

Mobile command vehicles were needed to help relief workers exchange information. In many places, telephone lines, cell phone towers, and other systems had been destroyed. The mobile command vehicles have equipment that sends communication via satellite.

Even with so many people there to help, New Orleans still looked like a war zone months after the hurricane. Despite these difficult conditions, law enforcement agencies had stopped criminals and had communicated important information so that relief workers could get on with the cleanup.

President Bush officially creates the Department of Homeland Security (DHS) on November 25, 2002. The Secret Service and the FPS became part of the new department.

A Tale of Two Services

President George W. Bush created the Department of Homeland Security (DHS) in 2001. It began operation on January 24, 2003. Many federal agencies were gathered together within the new department. Two of these organizations were the U.S. Secret Service and the Federal Protective Service (part of U.S. Immigration and Customs Enforcement).

The U.S. Secret Service (USSS) is charged with protecting the president of the United States and other government officials. The agency also investigates any criminal activity regarding U.S. currency or financial systems, from counterfeiting to Internet fraud.

The Federal Protective Service (FPS) guards federal properties and investigates criminal activity occurring on or near them. The FPS also supports other federal agencies by providing security for federal personnel upon request.

Each agency brings together special groups of law enforcement professionals and support personnel. As the agencies expand their roles, they are always looking for hardworking, conscientious men and women.

The USSS employs about 2,100 special agents, 1,200 Uniformed Division officers, and 1,700 other support personnel.[1] The support workers include technical, professional, and administrative staff. The USSS has a long history. It began in 1865 with just a few agents. These workers were charged with tracking down counterfeiters—criminals who print fake money. Today, the USSS is responsible for the lives of the nation's leaders. Its agents also protect the national currency and work to stop computer fraud. The USSS ensures that national events, such as presidential inaugurations, are safe. Its responsibilities have grown over nearly 150 years of serving the country.

The FPS is a far older service. Its roots are in the period just after the American Revolution (1775–1783). The FPS is responsible for the safety of workers in thousands of federal offices. It attends to any crime that happens on or near property owned by the federal government. FPS special agents investigate crimes ranging from drug sales to theft, murder, and kidnapping. Uniformed officers protect federal buildings and guard national events. They also safeguard disaster

FPS agents and local police officers arrive at the U.S. Federal Courthouse in Alexandria, Virginia. They work together to provide security for the trial of Zacarias Moussaoui, who was charged in the September 11 terrorist attacks.

teams during emergencies such as hurricanes and terrorist attacks. From trained dog-and-handler teams that locate bombs to inspectors who keep workplaces safe, the FPS has made a difference in the nation's wars on crime and terror.

Highly trained specialists with skills in many fields support the USSS and the FPS. Job requirements are demanding. The hours are often long, but there are many opportunities for success. The USSS and the FPS offer

unique career paths. They provide the opportunity to serve the country by fighting criminals and terrorists who seek to destroy Americans' freedoms.

The United States Secret Service: 140 Years of Protection

March 30, 1981, was sunny but chilly in Washington, D.C. President Ronald Reagan was leaving the Hilton Hotel after a speech to four thousand members of labor unions. The speech had gone well, and the president was in good humor. He joked with well-wishers who had gathered to see him. President Reagan was surrounded by Secret Service agents. He had learned to walk briskly while still taking time to wave and chat with a crowd.

Suddenly, a smiling, heavy-set young man with unruly hair stepped from the shadowed wall of the building. He raised his hand, holding a small .22 caliber revolver. The gun was loaded with explosive bullets. He fired as soon as the barrel came level. Squeezing the trigger again and again, he sprayed shots in the direction of the president.

There was no time to think or to plan a move—only to react as trained. Secret Service agent Timothy McCarthy stepped between the blasting pistol and his president. An explosive bullet struck the agent in the stomach and spun him around. Two other agents rushed to the president's side. They shoved him head-first into his limousine.

Chaos follows the 1981 shooting of President Reagan. Secret Service agent Timothy McCarthy (foreground), as well as a police officer and Reagan's press secretary James Brady, lie shot and wounded.

As the limousine sped away, agents and police wrestled would-be assassin John W. Hinckley, Jr., to the pavement. Then they quickly disarmed him. Others went to help wounded members of Reagan's party. Within a few blocks, agents discovered that a bullet had bounced off the car's rear door and hit President Reagan in the chest. With squealing tires and the shriek of brakes, the limousine swung toward George Washington University Hospital. Secret Service agents took the

As the limousine sped away, agents and police wrestled would-be assassin John W. Hinckley, Jr., to the pavement. Then they quickly disarmed him.

wounded president directly into the operating room. Looking around at the circle of doctors ready to operate, Reagan still had the energy to crack a joke. "I hope you're all Republicans," he said.[2]

During his recovery, President Reagan wrote to Agent McCarthy, who also had survived the attack. "There will always be a special gratitude I feel for your extraordinary heroism on that one cold day in March," wrote Reagan. "It is a gratitude words could never convey."[3]

The Secret Service agents in the Presidential Protective Division are the most visible workers of any federal law enforcement organization. They work at important events where national leaders are present. They can be seen on television and in newspapers. Yet these agents represent only a small fraction of the highly trained specialists who work for the USSS. Many of these specialists are invisible to the casual observer.

In 2006, special agents made up less than half of the almost 5,000 employees of the USSS. This might seem like a small number of employees, but the USSS is growing. Since the terrorist attacks of September 11, 2001, budgets for hiring have increased. It is not easy to get a job at the USSS. The agency has strict requirements for its employees. However, there are more opportunities than ever to serve in this respected law enforcement agency.

For people interested in working for the Secret Service, it is a good idea to know something about its history and traditions. Many events over the past 140 years have shaped its character.

A Brief History of the USSS

On July 5, 1865, the U.S. Secret Service Division was born out of a pressing need.[4] After the Civil War (1861–1865), the country was in financial trouble. There were huge war debts. Counterfeiters made this problem even worse. They flooded the marketplace with fake money.

By 1867, the officers of the new division were assigned to investigate any fraud that affected the federal government. Land swindlers, bootleggers making illegal whiskey, mail robbers, and smugglers all found themselves facing the Secret Service. In 1883, the service became part of the U.S. Treasury Department.

Government protection of the president began in 1894. That year, the Secret Service was asked to keep an eye on President Grover Cleveland. This protection only included public appearances. Agents did not watch the president around the clock as they do today. Up to that time, presidential security had been casual. Thomas Jefferson often answered the door himself, sometimes in a robe and slippers, when someone visited his home. The sixth president, John Quincy Adams, would leave the White House by himself early in the morning to go skinny-dipping in a nearby pond. The White House door was open to anyone coming to visit President Abraham Lincoln. Even after Lincoln's assassination in April 1865, guarding the president was not a priority.

Grover Cleveland was the Secret Service's first presidential protectee.

In September 1901, President William McKinley was shot in Buffalo, New York. This event sparked a

After President William McKinley was assassinated in 1901, the Secret Service began to protect U.S. presidents around the clock.

new era in presidential security. The Secret Service was given responsibility for the president's safety at all times. Later, this extended to the vice president and other government officials. Today, past presidents and their families are protected for life. However, President Bush and all who come after him will have a ten-year limit on the protection they receive. Foreign leaders are also granted Secret Service protection when they visit the United States.

The FPS: Law Enforcement with a Long Tradition

The Federal Protective Service began operation in 1790.[5] At that time, Congress authorized President George Washington to name three special commissioners. Their job was to select a location for the permanent home of the federal government. The new commissioners chose a tract of swampy land in Virginia. This land was named Washington in the District of Columbia. Buildings erected on the land became federal buildings, owned by the government. Four years later, six watchmen were hired to keep an eye on government warehouses. They patrolled with only a short club, called a cudgel, as a weapon. They carried oil lanterns at the top of tall staffs. These were the first FPS officers.

Governments tend to grow as the years go by. As they expand, they need more buildings to house politicians, personnel, judges, and agencies that run the country. In 1948, a corps of special agents was assigned to protect all buildings owned by the U.S. government. A year later, Congress transferred responsibility for government-owned property to the General Services Administration. The FPS force was known then as the U.S. Special Police. In 1971, the General Services Administration signed an official order to create the Federal Protective Force.

At first, the FPS was considered a security guard service. Officers were assigned to buildings at a fixed post. They did patrols to look for fire and safety hazards. They checked to make sure offices were locked. In fact, FPS agents were called door shakers because they rattled doors to make sure things were secure. They manned exits and entrances and answered visitors' questions. They tracked package deliveries and pickups. Actual police training was limited.

Things changed on April 19, 1995, at 9:02 A.M. That morning, Timothy McVeigh parked a rental truck

The blast blew off the front side of the nine-story building. More than 160 men, women, and children were killed.

at the Alfred P. Murrah Federal Building in Oklahoma City. Inside the truck was a bomb made from a deadly mixture of fertilizer and fuel packed in plastic. The bomb exploded, and the blast blew off the front side of the nine-story building. The force of the explosion collapsed floors. Victims were buried under concrete and steel. More than 160 men, women, and children were killed. Timothy McVeigh was put to death by lethal injection on June 11, 2001, as punishment for this terrible crime.

The Alfred P. Murrah Federal Building in Oklahoma City was hardly recognizable after the bombing on April 19, 1995.

The FPS changed its level of police training after the Oklahoma City bombing. The Department of Justice took a hard look at federal government properties that might be targets for violence or terrorism. A study done by several government agencies led to one main recommendation: The FPS had to be strengthened to deal with terrorist threats. It needed to take the lead in securing public buildings.

The FPS had to be strengthened to deal with terrorist threats.

With the destruction of the World Trade Center on September 11, 2001, it became even clearer that the FPS was vital to national security. The agency gained additional responsibility. Today more than ever, government buildings may be targets of serious crimes, including terrorism. In 2006, the FPS was in charge of security for more than 8,800 government-owned and government-leased facilities across the country.[6]

Secret Service special agents work on the front line of federal protection and law enforcement. They are responsible for the safety of the nation's top leaders.

Frontline Jobs with the United States Secret Service

Frontline jobs with the USSS involve two types of agents: special agents and Uniformed Division police officers. This chapter first discusses what it takes to become a special agent. Then it provides a look inside a career with the Uniformed Division.

Secret Service Special Agents

Secret Service special agents are among the most highly trained protection and investigation personnel in the world. Agents have developed what they call "the Look." They wear dark suits specially made to conceal their weapons. They talk into microphones hidden in their sleeves and look out at the public

This special agent demonstrates what the USSS calls "the Look"—dark sunglasses, dark suit, and a small earpiece, which is a part of a radio communication system.

through dark glasses. Yet they work hard to remain as inconspicuous as possible—especially when protecting the president. This job is known as the Presidential Protection Detail.

To begin the quest for a career as a special agent—or most jobs in the Secret Service—an applicant must be at least twenty-one years old and no older than thirty-seven. He or she must have either three years of law enforcement experience or a bachelor's degree. Preferred studies are in law, law enforcement, criminal justice, and psychology. Law enforcement in the military is another option. One agent said this about preparing for police work: "It sounds strange, but if you want to catch criminals, you have to learn to think like they do. Crimes make sense to the people who commit them. I have to be able to think like a criminal."[1]

Agents need to be physically fit. Fitness affects every part of their job. Agents have to work long hours, and getting tired is not an option. They must be able to run, to lift heavy objects, and to use weapons. They also

Special agents receive firearms training at the Federal Law Enforcement Training Center (FLETC).

need a sharp mind. An agent must be on the alert, ready to spring into action at any moment. One retiring agent noted, "Sixteen years in the Presidential Detail was like living coiled up in a jack-in-the-box."[2]

People interested in working for the USSS begin by filling out a job application and several other forms. The process continues with a background check and a drug screen. If an applicant has been convicted of a felony

President Bush (middle) watches a Secret Service training exercise at the James J. Rowley Training Center in Laurel, Maryland.

(a federal crime), the hiring process ends. A bonus of 25 percent of the agent's pay is offered to people who speak a foreign language fluently.

A Secret Service agent's training begins with eleven weeks of physical training and academic study at the Federal Law Enforcement Training Center (FLETC) in either Glynco, Georgia, or Artesian Wells, New Mexico. At FLETC, agents receive expert instruction in weapons use and physical defense. They also receive drivers' training. They learn about the law, psychology, and many other areas of study. Next comes eleven weeks of specialized instruction at the James J. Rowley Training Center in Laurel, Maryland.

Following the twenty-two weeks of training, new agents work at a field office in a major city. They start doing criminal investigation work. This allows the agents to work with experienced specialists at the agency and to learn new skills.

The USSS Financial Crimes Division Fights Computer Crime

In 2004, Secret Service agents ran a series of raids and caught twenty-eight criminals in seven countries. The criminals were guilty of computer fraud and identity theft. The agents were investigating cyber crime—using computers and technology to commit crimes. The investigation of cyber crime and identity theft has become an important part of the Secret Service Financial Crimes Division.

The 2004 arrests resulted from a Secret Service undercover operation. Agents worked to get inside a ring of identity theft, fraud, and forgery gangs. These criminals

Female Assassins: Two Attempts on President Ford's Life

When President Richard Nixon resigned in 1974, Vice President Gerald Ford became president. Two attempts were made on Ford's life while he greeted the public. On September 5, 1975, President Ford visited Sacramento, California. While he shook hands with a crowd of admirers, Lynette "Squeaky" Fromm, twenty-seven years old, aimed a pistol at the president's stomach. A fast-acting Secret Service agent thrust the webbing between his thumb and forefinger in front of the pistol's cocked hammer so the gun could not fire. Other agents wrestled Fromm to the ground.

Only seventeen days later, on September 22, a civil rights activist named Sara Jane Moore stood across the street from Ford's limousine (above). As Ford was about to enter the car, she drew a revolver. Bystander Oliver Sipple saw the weapon. He knocked the gun upward as Moore fired. Secret Service agents shoved the president into the car and roared away. Other agents and bystanders stopped Moore before any more shots could be fired. Both Fromm and Moore are now serving life sentences in prison.

traded confidential information about people online. The thieves stole more than 1.7 million credit card numbers. They forged driver's licenses, birth certificates, and other types of identification. These documents could be used illegally to open false bank accounts or to get a credit card in another person's name. Bank losses through credit card fraud were estimated at $4.3 million.

The Secret Service fights telecommunication fraud. Losses caused by this type of crime are estimated at more than $1 billion each year.

The Financial Crimes Division investigates illegal electronic funds transfer (transfer of money over the Internet), theft of U.S. Treasury bonds, and forgery. It also coordinates and oversees money-laundering investigations. For example, it fights telecommunication fraud. Losses caused by this type of crime are estimated at more than $1 billion each year. One of the largest markets for telecommunication fraud is the cloning of cellular telephones. Cloning transfers the electronic serial number of a stolen cell phone to other cell phones. This allows a user to charge calls to the owner of the stolen phone. It is a federal offense.

The United States PATRIOT Act was passed on October 26, 2001. This law increased the Secret Service's role in securing U.S. financial payment systems—that is, the transfer of money to pay for products or services. The Secret Service also fights international financial crimes. This is the theft of money sent from one country to another by terrorists or other criminals. For example, a criminal deposits illegal drug money into a bank. Then a computer transfers the money to a foreign bank. Later this same money is transferred back to the United States, this time to a different bank. The money has been illegally laundered, or washed clean, of all connection with the original money made from selling drugs.

Investigations of financial crimes can take months. They require patience and the ability to connect many pieces of evidence. USSS agents need to create a solid case that will stand up in a court of law. To help solve cases, the Secret Service needs to cooperate with local law enforcement agencies all across the country. Investigators also must be able to work well with others.

Secret Service Protection

The earliest work of the USSS did not involve protection of national leaders. This responsibility has evolved since Richard Lawrence aimed a pistol at President Andrew Jackson in 1835 and pulled the trigger. The pistol misfired. Lawrence produced another pistol and tried again. The second gun also misfired. Lawrence was taken to an insane asylum.

After this attempted assassination, a guardhouse was built on the front lawn of the White House. To this day, a guard is always there to stand watch. As one of his last official acts before his assassination, President Lincoln gave the secretary of the treasury permission to officially create the Secret Service.

Today the Secret Service forms a bubble that surrounds any public person the agency must protect. This person is called a protectee. Agents who are assigned to the Presidential Protective Division (PPD)

Today the Secret Service forms a bubble that surrounds any public person the agency must protect.

perform the main task of the U.S. Secret Service. The PPD is responsible for the personal security of the president and the president's family. Its agents provide protectees with round-the-clock protection.

The PPD also conducts advance security for presidential trips and major events. What does this involve? First, teams of specialists visit the location of an event and the streets leading to and from it. They check the physical layout of any place the president will go. They run background checks on every person who will come in contact with the

The elite special agents on a Counter Assault Team (CAT) are trained to stop attacks against high-profile U.S. leaders.

president and his party. This includes anyone from hotel clerks and waiters to government employees and local police.

The PPD includes a special unit called the Counter Assault Team (CAT). The CAT was created in the late 1970s. It became part of the USSS in 1992. The CAT relies on select special agents to stop an attack on a protectee as quickly as possible. The PPD also includes the Emergency Response Team (ERT).

The ERT units respond to security problems on the White House grounds. What kind of situation might require the ERT's skills? If a person jumps the White House fence or if a car crashes into it, ERT agents are called to the scene. In a more serious case, the ERT would respond if a person shot a gun at the White House. ERT teams are made up of specially trained members of the other frontline branch of the USSS—the Uniformed Division.

The Uniformed Division of the USSS

Since about 1860, the government relied on the military and the Washington, D.C., police force to

Members of an Emergency Response Team (ERT) quickly catch someone who has jumped the White House fence.

The Attack on President Truman

On November 1, 1950, President Harry S. Truman was living with his wife and daughter at the Blair House in Washington, D.C., while the White House was being remodeled. At that time, Puerto Rico was demanding separation from the United States to become an independent country. Two Puerto Ricans who believed in the cause approached Blair House. Two members of the White House Police were guarding the steps to the front door.

The two men drew their pistols and rushed the stairs. They fired wildly to shoot their way past the guards and kill the president. At the top of the stairs, facing a hail of bullets, was Secret Service Agent Leslie Coffelt, a uniformed policeman. He fired one shot. It killed assassin Griselio Torresola and sent him rolling back down the stairs. Other police arrived. Two were wounded before the second assassin, Oscar Collazo (above), fell. In only a few seconds, the two gunmen were dead. At the top of the steps, Officer Coffelt had been hit. He soon died of his wounds. He was the first casualty of what became the Uniformed Division of the Secret Service.

protect the president and the president's family. Then, in 1922, President Warren G. Harding created the White House Police Force. The effectiveness of the force was questioned several years later. An unknown man managed to wander into the White House one evening to have a chat with President Herbert Hoover in the dining room. This event made it clear that tougher security was needed. In 1930, President Hoover reassigned the authority of the White House Police to the Secret Service.

The uniform service worked as the Executive Protective Division and other names before it became the U.S. Secret Service Uniformed Division in 1977. The division includes three branches: the Administration and Support Branch, the Foreign Mission Branch, and the White House Branch.

Uniformed Division police officers are trained in a variety of police tasks. Their main job, though, is the protection of the president and the president's family while they are at the White House. The division also provides protection at the home of the vice president and the vice president's family. It protects foreign diplomats in the Washington area and the offices of the vice president as well. Uniformed officers patrol their assigned areas either in vehicles or on foot. The Uniformed Division also provides support to other parts of the Secret Service through the use of K-9 (dog) units, counter-sniper teams, and other specialized forces.

FLETC: The Federal Law Enforcement Training Center

FLETC offers basic and advanced police training to several government agencies. It also provides training especially for an agency's needs. Many of its instructors are long-time officers with years of experience. FLETC is the federal government's main provider of law enforcement courses.[3]

FLETC has several modern training facilities. It uses state-of-the-art police training equipment to help its students gain top skills. Among the latest courses are the counterterrorism programs. These programs educate students about the following topics:

- **bombs and explosives**
- **detection of weapons and explosives**
- **crisis management**—how to remain calm during an emergency and to follow certain procedures to ensure the safety of others
- **patrol procedures**—how to patrol an area, on foot or in a vehicle, to ensure that the area and people in the area are secure
- **physical security**—how to check the security of exits and entrances, offices, and equipment and to protect them from theft, fire, or damage
- **tactical applications**—use of personnel and equipment to control a situation that might cause harm
- **transportation security**
- **building and room searches**
- **weapons of mass destruction**

- **arrest warrants**—procedures to follow when seeking legal permission to make an arrest
- **personal protection**—use of bulletproof vests, weapons, chemical sprays, batons, shields, and helmets; teaching officers to support each other during riot control; being aware of the patrol environment at all times
- **first response**—what officers must do when they are the first to arrive at the scene of an emergency
- **hazardous materials**—the use of special equipment, clothing, and procedures to lower the risk from dangerous chemicals and other substances

FLETC also operates the James J. Rowley Training Center in Laurel, Maryland. Agents and officers learn how to use high-tech equipment at the center. They are also trained in counterterrorism and security procedures.

To join the Uniformed Division, applicants must be U.S. citizens between the ages of twenty-one and thirty-seven. They must have a valid driver's license. They must pass a written examination and possess a high school diploma or the equivalent. A complete physical examination is required, as are a strict background investigation and complete drug screen. Applicants also go through several interviews with USSS officials.

Once they meet these basic requirements, recruits attend eight weeks of training in police procedures at FLETC. After that, they undergo eleven more weeks of training at the James J. Rowley Training Center in Laurel, Maryland.

After earning their badges, Uniformed Division officers are assigned to protect one of the following:

- the White House Complex, the U.S. Treasury building, and other presidential offices
- the president and members of the president's immediate family
- the official residence of the vice president in the District of Columbia
- the vice president and members of the vice president's immediate family
- foreign diplomatic missions throughout the United States, its territories, and its possessions
- the political conventions for the presidency during election years (other agencies also attend to this task)

Weapons of the Secret Service

All special agents and Uniformed Division officers go through firearms training with the weapons that they will use in the field. The official handgun of the Secret Service is the SIG Sauer P229 semiautomatic pistol. It holds twelve ammunition rounds in its magazine. Agents and officers also use the Remington 870 short-barrel shotgun with up to four loads in the magazine. Each buckshot load includes eight pellets that spread out after leaving the barrel. To fight terrorists or criminals who use machine guns, Secret Service agents and officers are trained to fire the Heckler & Koch MP-5 submachine gun with fifteen- or thirty-round box magazines. It fires at a rate of eight hundred rounds per minute.

Uniformed Division officers wear white shirts, neckties, and dark slacks when guarding public areas. When guarding against snipers or in other dangerous situations, the officers wear heavy laced boots and body armor. They carry semiautomatic pistols and other equipment needed to keep the peace. The officers do their jobs with the help of special USSS support units, including the counter-sniper and ERT units described earlier.

Uniformed counter-sniper teams include an expert rifleman using a heavy .308 caliber Remington Model 700 rifle with a telescopic sight. The rifle may also have starlight night-vision capability to help the agent see in the dark. The rifleman works with another trained rifleman acting as a spotter. This person keeps constant watch over his or her assigned area with high-power binoculars. These riflemen must regularly prove their ability to shoot accurately on the rifle range. Their job depends on their exceptional skills.

A variety of weapons are available to agents and officers when necessary. They might use smoke grenades and concussion flash-bang grenades, which emit a burst of fire and smoke with a loud "Bang!" Shotguns, automatic weapons, and two-way radios also help them do their jobs.

Like special agents, the officers of the Uniformed Division must be ready at any time to defend and protect their assigned post and the people who live and work there. Every trained move must be done without delay. As one veteran uniformed officer said, "We wear uniforms and carry guns in plain sight. We're a lot like city police, except our home base city is Washington, D.C.—a city full of important people.

"Officially, uniformed officers don't need bachelor's degrees, but there's never an end to the applicants. The

A USSS counter-sniper rifleman prepares to guard President Bush on his visit to an Arizona Diamondbacks baseball game in 2005.

Earning Power on the Secret Service Front Line

The General Schedule, or GS, sets the level of pay for government employees. It changes every January when Congress votes on which workers will get raises. For example, in 2006, a special agent or Uniformed Division officer working in Atlanta, Georgia, started at about $29,000 per year. He or she could reach roughly $43,000 per year over time. Supervisory jobs pay a higher rate up to $105,000 per year.

Special agents are often moved to new posts. Some cities are more expensive to live in than others, so cost-of-living bonuses are granted. For example, an agent in Chicago gets a 14.58 percent increase over the standard pay. An agent working in New York City receives 16 percent over the base salary.

Employees who have law enforcement duties receive Law Enforcement Availability Pay. They receive 25 percent over their base pay to cover times when they are called out in the middle of the night or have to work long hours on an investigation.

service only hires the very best candidates. If you want my job, go to college."[4]

Considering his years on the job as an officer with the Uniformed Division, one Secret Service veteran noted, "I've had a ringside seat at a lot of history. We protect foreign embassies and a lot of historic events, but you have to be alert at all times. How could an assassin get at someone I'm protecting? Was that door open the last time I walked by? If I have only one second to make a life and death decision, I can't take two seconds."[5]

Hard Work—Both Dangerous and Rewarding

Being a special agent or a Uniformed Division officer is a dangerous way to make a living. Yet most of the time, the job depends on routines—the same things done over and over again. There are boring hours of waiting, traveling in airplanes, living out of a suitcase in hotels, and grabbing quick meals.

A Secret Service employee gives over his or her life to the job. This includes decisions about where to live, when to travel, and how many hours to work each day. Secret Service employees must be just as professional guarding a political leader whose policies they do not agree with as they are with one they respect and admire. For some agents, an entire twenty-year career might roll past without a dangerous event. They never fire a weapon in the line of duty, and they arrive home safely at the end of the day. Even so, it is a career that offers a sense of purpose and responsibility—a job that makes a difference.

FPS officers work to ensure public safety at the Republican National Convention in New York City in 2004.

Frontline Jobs with the Federal Protective Service

An FPS special agent sat with other agents and watched television monitors. The "show" on the screens was one they had watched for many nights. Now the program was coming to an end. Tape recorders hummed their electronic buzz. Reels turned, and the images on the screens were recorded. Almost showtime. The agent checked the magazine in his SIG Sauer P229 .357 magnum semiautomatic pistol. He never knew how these busts would go down. One wrong word, one wrong move, and everything could go wrong in the blink of an eye.

"High-ranking officials had made complaints to our office that drugs were being sold in and around a federal property," the agent says. "We set up surveillance and then called in some uniform officers to dress in

An FPS car sits in front of the Peachtree Summit building in Atlanta, Georgia. The agency protects nearly nine thousand federal properties.

plain clothes and make some drug buys. We wanted to see the actual hand-to-hand sales, so we set up hidden video cameras."

Day after day, the undercover FPS officers played their roles and bought drugs from the dealers. A restaurant and nightclub bordered the federal property. The cameras showed that the dealers were getting their drugs from that business.

"The local police sergeant and I decided on a joint operation to make a stronger case and to pool our manpower."

"I was team leader for the operation," the agent continues. "When we had enough taped transactions, I followed our usual procedure and called in the local police to help with the arrests. I was surprised to find out they had the same location under surveillance for drug trafficking. The local police sergeant and I decided on a joint operation to make a stronger case and to pool our manpower."

The FPS special agent took the tapes and other evidence to his commander for approval to make arrests. FPS control extends from federal property to any bordering property. The joint team met before dark and made sure everyone knew his or her job.

Forty FPS and local police officers closed in on the property and began rounding up the drug dealers. Red, blue, and white lights flashed. Commands were shouted. Handcuffs were swiftly snapped around wrists. There was no place to run for the bewildered dealers. Another group of officers forced their way into the restaurant and seized the dealers' supplies. Customers were escorted out, and the restaurant's owners joined the line of offenders filing into police vans.

Forty FPS and local police officers closed in on the property and began rounding up the drug dealers. Red, blue, and white lights flashed.

"We did it one night and made thirteen or fourteen arrests besides shutting down the restaurant," the agent says. "No one was hurt, and no more drug sales were ever made there. That's a perfect operation."[1]

Patrol and Investigator Jobs with the FPS

FPS officers' primary job of protecting federal property and employees has not changed over the years. The scope of FPS work and responsibility has grown, however. Now it includes a full range of police powers. These include investigative work, emergency communication, crowd control, monitoring safety conditions, and establishing security rules for federal properties.

The frontline jobs with FPS are broken down into the following positions:

- special agents (criminal investigators)
- federal uniformed police officers
- FPS inspectors

Training for these officers includes eight weeks of instruction at FLETC in Glynco, Georgia. This is the same basic program as that of the USSS explained in Chapter 3. From that point on, officers take special courses depending on their chosen fields and past education. Four FPS officers spoke about their careers for this book. (Their first names are used here for security purposes.) They offer an inside look at what it is like to work for the FPS.

FPS Special Agents—Criminal Investigators

FPS criminal investigators serve in plain clothes as armed special agents. They investigate felonies, make arrests, gather criminal intelligence, and work with other law enforcement officials. They search for and preserve evidence at crime scenes.

Special agents participate in Federal Task Forces. These are crime-fighting groups put together from many agencies to work on a single crime or a series of crimes. They must be able to do surveillance and to conduct interviews. Then they present the results of their investigations to U.S. attorneys. These are the lawyers who will try cases in court. Special agents are often called to testify in court. Today's agents are also trained to predict possible terrorist acts.

Agent Cleo is a supervisor and criminal investigator with the FPS. He supervises special agents in six states. He has worked in law enforcement since he left high school. Agent Cleo was the key figure in the drug bust that opened this chapter.

"I joined the army right out of high school and went into the military police," Cleo says. "While I was an MP [military policeman], I took college courses and joined the army's Criminal Investigation Division (CID). It was the start of a long line of schools starting with the MP Academy and CID School and including FBI courses at Quantico, Virginia, and even correction officer training as a prison guard—but at the time, I'd never heard of the FPS."

Agent Cleo stayed in the army for five years. He took as much time as possible to learn the trade of criminal investigation. When he was ready to return to civilian life, his education and military record put him in high demand.

"The military can help you get into law enforcement. The local police require an associate [two-year] college degree to join the department. You can also join if you have four years in the military. If you can do four years in the military, you can go anywhere in the world and work in law enforcement. I made sergeant in less than

Weapons of the FPS

Every agent, uniformed officer, or inspector who joins the FPS must train in the use of a wide range of weapons. They must also recertify their skills on a regular basis, usually every three months. The responsibility of carrying a loaded weapon in public areas weighs heavily on every officer. If the weapon is discharged for any reason, a report must be filed, and the shooting will be investigated.

The weapons assigned to FPS officers cover a wide range of situations. During their training at FLETC, they learn to use their handgun, which is with them at all times when on duty. Today, agents and officers face criminals with very powerful guns. Now the FPS uses the SIG Sauer P229 in .357 SIG caliber.

Agents on patrol also have access to shoulder-type weapons. These include the Remington 870 shotgun with an eighteen-inch barrel and the M4 military rifle (below)—a shorter version of the M16. For even more firepower, the Fabrique Nationale (Belgium) P90 submachine gun is available. It fires a 5.7-mm bullet at nine hundred shots per minute. Agents must requalify with these weapons four times a year. Law enforcement officers who fire a gun in a public place are responsible for every bullet and where it strikes. Only the highest level of training is good enough.

two years in the service. Law enforcement agencies can look at your military records and see your commitment and skill levels in black and white. And you can also get here through college taking criminal justice and law enforcement courses.

"The state police, local police, the state prisons, and the Federal Protective Service all wanted me. It was a tough choice, but two factors pointed to the FPS. First, I could stay in my hometown, and, second,

Over the last few years, Agent Cleo has investigated cases of theft, arson, assault and battery, illegal drug sale and use, and even homicide.

my five years in the military would count toward my eventual retirement since I would still be a federal employee. FPS sent me to the eight-week course at FLETC, and I started out as a uniformed federal police officer. That only lasted six months, and I was sent back to FLETC for the twelve-week Criminal Investigation Course."

Over the last few years, Agent Cleo has investigated cases of theft, arson, assault and battery, illegal drug sale and use, and even homicide. He is trained in voice stress analysis. This technique involves using a computer to measure tremors in the voice. These tremors can indicate whether a person is lying during the recording of a statement or testimony.

Agent Cleo is also on one of six squads of the Federal Bureau of Investigation's (FBI) Federal Joint Terrorist Task Force. He plays an active role in counterterrorism. He helps the force track down information to begin investigations of possible terrorist activity. Besides the Federal Protective Service, the task force consists of local and county police; the U.S. Secret Service; the Bureau of Alcohol, Tobacco, Firearms and Explosives; the FBI; and the U.S. Marshals Service. The combined resources of this group can follow any investigation from beginning to end.

Taking on the job of FPS special agent requires constant retraining and learning new skills. "I have to keep my training up to date," Agent Cleo says. "That means Terrorist Alert Training every five years. Every three years I have to take a legal update course and every two years recertify my voice stress qualification. Every two to five years, I go back to FLETC for interrogation school, and at three-month intervals, I have to recertify my firearms skills. Depending on the weapons I have assigned to me, I have to recertify my skill with each one.

"We deal with armed robberies in restaurants and shops within buildings that are government facilities," Agent Cleo says. "The lobby newsstand, restaurants, clothing stores, bookstores, any shops, banks, or boutiques on the premises become our case. We even get kidnappings from day-care centers on federal property. As the government buys building

"My investigators can work a case if something is stolen or vandalized that is valued at more than $1,000—the federal guideline for a felony."

locations, our responsibilities increase. My investigation threshold right now is $1,000. My investigators can work a case if something is stolen or vandalized that is valued at more than $1,000—the federal guideline for a felony. [For] anything worth less than $1,000, we turn the case over to the uniformed federal police officer, or inspectors work the case with our help."

The FPS is the police department for the federal government. If a crime is committed in an FBI building, it calls FPS. Even if this property is simply a tent, or if employees have federal government property stolen from their house, it is an FPS case.

Agent Cleo explains, "I could use another ten agents to cover all the work. The FPS is always looking for good people. Everybody brings something different to the table. Besides their assigned work, everybody has a chance to develop certain specialties."

FPS officers in uniform, along with their canine helpers, work to protect the federal government at its numerous locations across the country.

The salary for FPS criminal investigators begins at around $27,500. This rate is higher if the agent is assigned to a more expensive city. The pay varies according to the cost of living. Top pay is about $140,000. Supervisors start at about $72,000.

"If it affects the government, we can investigate it," Agent Cleo says. "Cases aren't solved in an hour episode, like on TV. Some cases take a day, and some take years to close. I do this job because I like to help people. When I get a case where a person is injured or robbed, I like to know I make a difference. I've got ten more years before I retire to make a difference," he says proudly.[2]

FPS Uniformed Officers

On August 18, 2004, a family had just finished business at the Bloomington, Minnesota, office of the Department of Homeland Security. They noticed their son was having difficulty breathing. Paramedics were called. The parents rushed the boy to the elevator. On the ground floor, they encountered FPS Sergeant Amy Kroth. By now, the child's condition had become worse. Sergeant Kroth checked the boy for a pulse and found none. Without hesitation, she began to perform CPR (cardiopulmonary resuscitation) and kept at it until she detected a pulse. She quickly shifted to mouth-to-mouth resuscitation and kept the boy breathing until the paramedics arrived.

"Sergeant Kroth's actions were nothing short of heroic," said Ronald Chamberlain, FPS area commander in Minnesota. "When the emergency arose, she didn't hesitate. I have no doubt that the child is alive today because of her actions."[3]

"You learn a lot of things in school that you may never use," said Kroth after the event. "But I've

Uniformed police officers are the backbone of the Federal Protective Service.

always thought lifesaving skills might come in handy." Kroth said the event had a special importance for her. She has a toddler herself. "I went home that night and held him for two hours straight," she said.[4]

Uniformed police officers are the backbone of the Federal Protective Service. They patrol federal properties night and day. They are on call to contribute their skills to any emergency—such as Hurricane Katrina—where federal employees are working. They also help local police upon request. They are, in every sense, the federal police force.

Officer George is a veteran with the FPS. He came into law enforcement from a troubled life as a young man. "I got kicked out of two high schools and was working on the docks," says Officer George. "I was eighteen years old and working on the south side of the city where there were plenty of gangs. My family told me to straighten myself out, so I joined the Marines. I needed some structure in my life and discipline. The Marines gave me plenty of that. Most of my friends back in the neighborhood ended up in jail. I think I made the right choice."

Officer George began a life in the military. He spent three years in the Marines fighting in developing nations and in Operation Desert Storm. "Seeing the world with an M16 rifle on my shoulder made me appreciate my country and what we have," he says. After leaving the Marines, he joined the U.S. Army National Guard. "I decided to return to civilian life, and of the outfits I contacted (the U.S. Border Patrol, the U.S. Marshals, the FPS, and the local police), it was the FPS that called me first."

Officer George did his three months of training at FLETC and began his fourteen-year tour with the FPS. It was in 2005 that he faced his greatest challenge. "I'd covered political conventions and other

Many FPS officers begin their careers in the U.S. Armed Forces. Officer George fought in the Marines during Operation Desert Storm (1990–1991).

national events which were a lot of work, but then came Hurricane Katrina. I spent thirty-four days in New Orleans. We were requested when Federal Emergency Management Agency's Disaster Medical Assistance Teams (DMAT) needed security while trying to help the refugees in the flooded city."

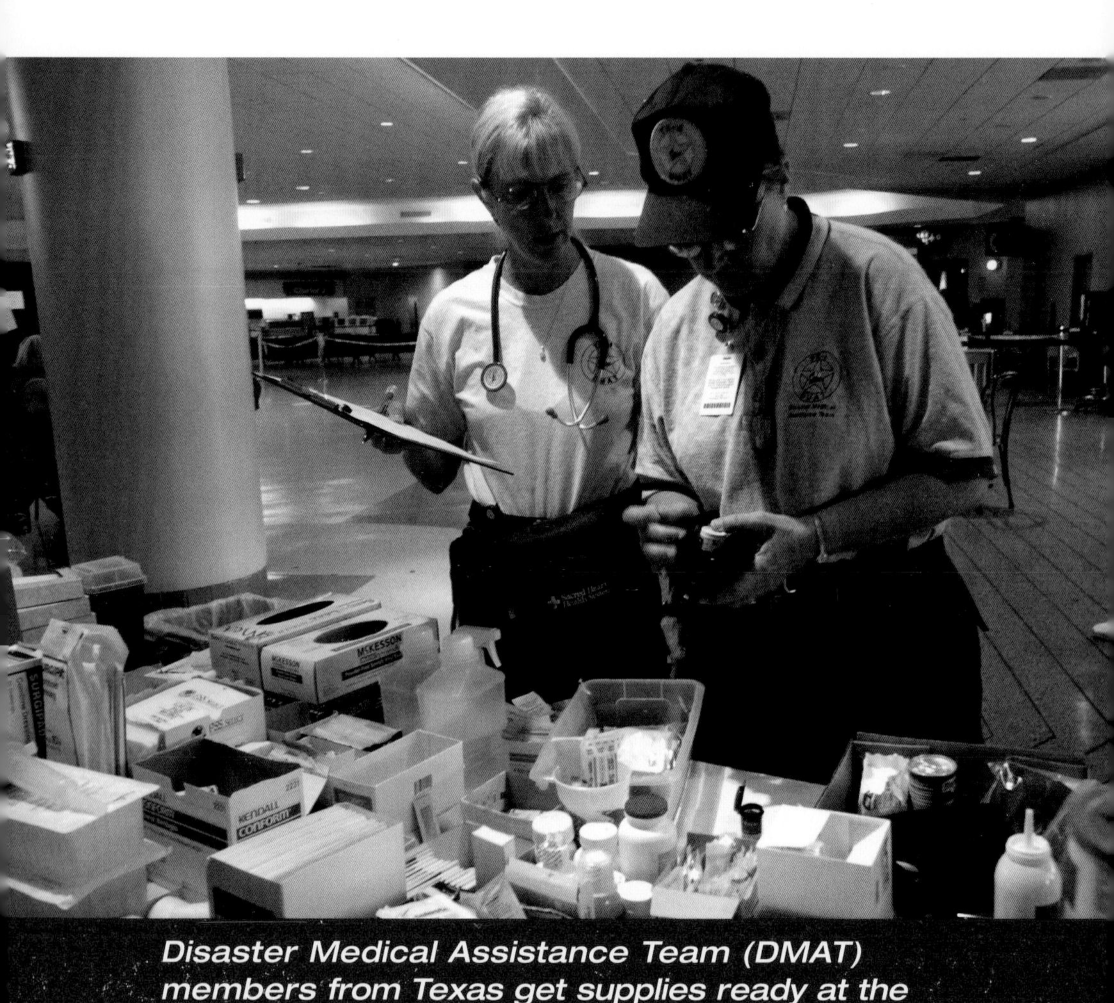

Disaster Medical Assistance Team (DMAT) members from Texas get supplies ready at the New Orleans airport after Hurricane Katrina.

DMAT teams are made up of volunteer doctors and nurses who rush to emergency situations. Each team has thirty-five support technicians and seventy-five medical personnel. Officer George recalls, "Region 5 [Ohio, Indiana, Illinois, Wisconsin, Michigan, and Minnesota] sent fifteen FPS personnel to New Orleans. We had seventy-five FPS officers in Louisiana in forty-eight hours.

"My team drove in SUVs for sixteen hours to get there," Officer George recalls. "I remembered when we were called out for the Trade Center collapse on September 11, 2001. We have to be ready to load up and be on the move any time of day or night."

The FPS unit set up a command post at Baton Rouge, Louisiana. Gangs looking for drugs overran a DMAT team. The FPS had to restore security so the team could work. The FPS had no GPS—global positioning satellite, which pinpoints a location by

The New Orleans evacuees were scared. Only having the FPS officers there in their uniforms helped calm the situation.

satellite—and no cell phones. They had to use maps found at gas stations to find their way around.

The Chicago Group had one FPS team in the Superdome, where people who had lost their homes were gathering. These evacuees had no belongings. They were scared. Only having the FPS officers there in their uniforms helped calm the situation. Another FPS team was at the airport. Its job was to search evacuees for weapons before they boarded planes to leave the city. The FPS team took away a pile of weapons that people had kept because they were frightened of the gangs and looters.

"Most of us FPS officers were former military," says Officer George, "and New Orleans was like being in a combat zone. I had great respect for the DMAT teams. We had weapons, but they were doctors and nurses, just going in on faith and to do their jobs."

The biggest problem for the FPS was dealing with the criminal element. Thugs and gang members had broken into gun stores and had stolen every weapon they could carry. At one point the FPS had to back up a SWAT (Special Weapons and Tactics) team that had cornered some thugs firing guns at officers on a bridge.

Officer George says, "We made some drug busts and later helped reduce sniper fire from rooftops where gangs had taken over whole neighborhoods."

FPS police officers were helping get elderly people to care facilities and transporting kids with diabetes to places where they could get help. They provided humanitarian help as well as protection. Officer George says, "In the field, we worked with other FPS administrative people—for instance, we were living out of our cars when we first arrived and had no communications. Our FPS support people got us the 'beans, bullets, and band-aids' we needed: lodging, food, supplies—all that had to be arranged from back here in the office or we couldn't have done our jobs."

"We're not just guards," Officer George explains. "The training we get at FLETC is the best in the world. They have the best instructors. I believe with all my

FPS Mobile Command Vehicles

FPS mobile command vehicles (MCVs) serve as high-tech communication centers for multiple law enforcement agencies. These large, forty-foot trailers cost about $400,000 each. MCVs are equipped to operate as radio base stations that connect portable radios into a network. The station allows law enforcement officials in various places to communicate with each other as they do their jobs. MCVs can also receive signals from video cameras. This ability to capture video signals, including aircraft video, allows commanders to monitor emergencies and criminal activities before sending in officers and equipment. MCVs' satellite communication links the computers of the FPS and other law enforcement agencies.

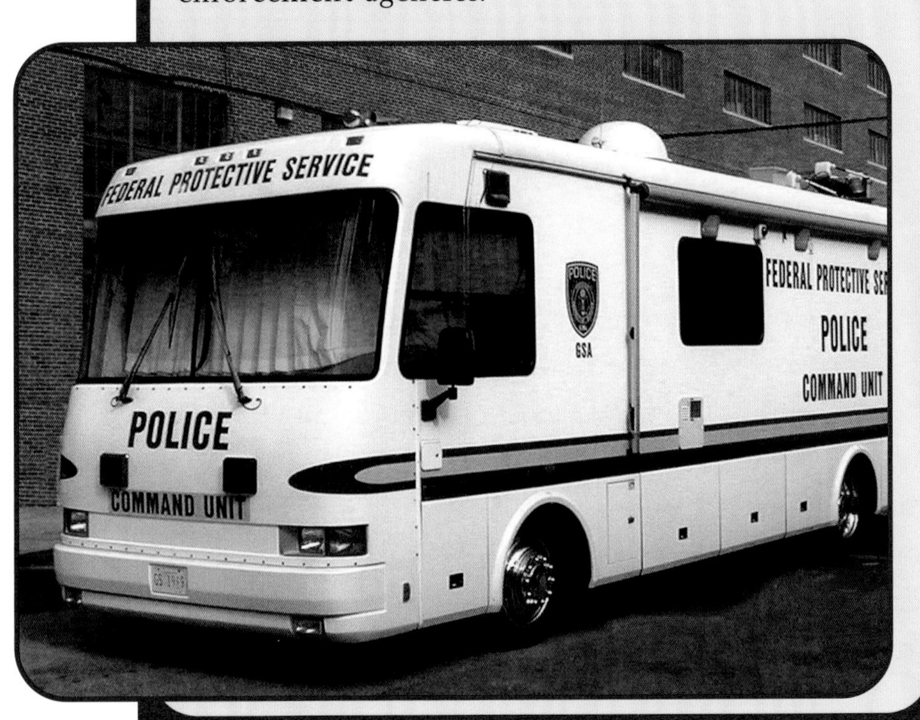

heart and soul that when I train my people, they understand that when the balloon goes up, everyone looks to you. I know I did my best to prepare them."

A normal salary for a starting FPS officer is $27,500. Officers can move up through the ranks to $41,700. Then they may become an officer lieutenant at $50,500, or they might even move on to captain at a salary of $60,500.

FPS candidates can be hired immediately after college graduation. Serving in the military is a bonus, but interviewers also ask about a candidate's work experience. Three years' experience in law enforcement or a degree in criminal law enforcement is a good beginning to a career in the service.

"Working with the FPS has given me a great sense of service," concludes Officer George. "You save lives and serve your country. I'm happy to be there when I'm needed. Of course, we have boring days when nothing happens—just patrols. But that can change in an instant. The training prepares you for that."[5]

FPS Inspectors: Setting Safe Standards

FPS Inspector Elizabeth is a one-year rookie, but she already thinks the FPS was a smart career move. "I went with a friend to a criminal justice job fair," Inspector Elizabeth says. "We filled out forms at the FPS booth and were called to apply. I think we had an edge because there were very few females in FPS. I also speak fluent Spanish, and a second language is a real bonus.

"We started in FPS as part-time paid interns doing a variety of jobs. This is called a co-op program. You have to be in college to apply. If you work well and earn your bachelor's degree in criminal justice, you are asked to stay. I also did public policy research in the city. And it helped that I picked my criminal justice major early while I was still in high school. I did a lot of work on the side as a community activist in nonprofit organizations. I love working with people—doing a lot of social work."

Inspector Elizabeth is a law enforcement officer. Her main responsibility is planning and monitoring security in federal Social Security and Internal Revenue Service offices. Her second responsibility is as a physical security specialist.

"It's my job to inspect and create a report on a facility's security weaknesses and strengths," she says. "When there's a new federal space proposed, we survey the area, look at crime statistics in the neighborhood, talk to the local police and neighborhood businesses, and build a picture of what security precautions might be needed. If it's a two-person operation like a recruiting office, the vulnerabilities are less. If it has a lot of computers, personnel, or cash on the premises, the security must be tighter. Each assessment is developed case by case."

FPS inspectors are trained for their jobs in the field. Some types of federal facilities require more skills than others. After basic training at FLETC, inspectors attend a four-week classroom academy. While there, they also work with other inspectors at smaller facilities with fewer employees and less serious security concerns. Federal facilities are classified in levels according to how large or important they are, as follows:

- A Level 5 facility requires extremely tight security. One Level 5 example is the Pentagon, the headquarters of the U.S. Department of Defense. The Pentagon has its own security staff.
- Level 4 is any high-rise federal building or several buildings in the same complex.
- Level 3 is a facility such as the ICE Headquarters in Oak Brook Terrace, Illinois. The building has an area of about 77,000 square feet and has many entrances.
- Level 2 would be a Social Security office with twenty-five employees who serve from sixty to one hundred applicants a day.
- Level 1 would be a U.S. Army recruiting office or a two-person office.

"Our first year," Inspector Elizabeth says, "we were tasked with several Level 1 and Level 2 offices. The next year we worked up to Level 3, and so on. We work with the inspectors here, and we are reviewed by area commanders. Everything has to be perfect." For example, she checks to make sure the closed-circuit TV cameras and alarm systems are working properly throughout the FPS Mega Center in Battle Creek, Michigan. Inspector Elizabeth explains, "That center handles about five or six states. If an alarm goes off in a Chicago suburb, the Mega Center tips off the local police or us depending on who is nearest the site to respond to that location."

The Pentagon in Arlington, Virginia, is a Level 5 federal facility. This means it requires the highest possible level of security.

Communication Mega Centers

Mega Centers monitor all types of alarm systems, closed-circuit television, and wireless communications within federal facilities nationwide. They provide alarm monitoring twenty-four hours a day, seven days a week. In the event of a partial or total failure at one center, all operations can be remotely switched and monitored at a sister location. Officers in the field can contact Mega Centers with their personal radios if they are anywhere in the area that their center serves. The centers can then call for help from the nearest emergency or law enforcement agency.

Inspector Elizabeth made $47,000 last year, including overtime. She expects to earn over $50,000 with cost-of-living and other bonuses. "It's a great job. You get to do a little bit of everything. I really enjoy the assessment work. I also like the law enforcement work. You make a difference—a positive action. You learn every day." [6]

FPS Inspector K-9 Dog Handlers

Discovering explosives is an important part of federal security. The FPS is now training inspector volunteers in this important field. Inspector Melissa is a long-time law enforcement officer. Today she has a new partner.

"I have what they call a single-purpose dog," says Inspector Melissa, "a bomb [explosives] detection dog.

> The sight of bomb-sniffing dogs is a reassuring sign that law enforcement is doing its job.

He's a black Labrador retriever named Shadow, weighs about seventy-two pounds, and is very happy with what he does. I've always had a love of animals but never had the opportunity to work with them.

"A typical day for me starts with exercising my dog. I set up what is called an open-air problem for him to solve using a training aid. If he finds it, he gets a reward. I play with him. Then we go into the city and patrol around the federal building complex. Sometimes I take Shadow down into the subway system that's around and under the buildings."

Subway and other mass-transit systems are targets for terrorist bombs and other types of attacks. The sight of bomb-sniffing dogs is a reassuring sign that law enforcement is doing its job. These counterterrorist canines check any unattended backpacks, trash containers, and packages left on benches and in other areas for dangerous explosives.

When Shadow makes a discovery, Inspector Melissa may work with local law enforcement officers to bring in a suspect. She explains, "If I need to make an arrest and I'm not on a federal property, I call the local police to assist. This provides the local jurisdiction [authority] that makes the arrest official. We have about two hundred federal facilities in the city area.

"When I signed up as a dog handler, I was introduced to Shadow. I'm responsible for his care and rewarding him when he does well. Next comes learning to 'read' the dog. You train with a particular dog and keep that dog when you graduate. You and the dog learn together. There are two weeks of classroom work and ten weeks of training."

The handler is introduced to the dog in the first week at the Auburn University Canine Detection Training Center in McClellan, Alabama. From then on, she or he is responsible for feeding the dog, cleaning his kennel, and walking him. Soon the dog realizes the handler is the person to turn to for everything in his day-to-day life—both work and play.

"You learn the dog's behavior so you are able to really understand what he's doing at any time," says Inspector Melissa. "If you don't understand why the dog is doing a particular thing, you might miss some important behavior when the dog is actually doing his job. They are trained to sniff the odor of an explosive, trace the odor to its source, and then sit. That is called a passive alert. You can't have a bomb-detection dog digging where he finds the explosive, or he may set it off. In a perfect world they're supposed to sit. Sometimes they get very excited. Shadow is very hyper, intense, focused—a fantastic sniffer."

Bomb-Sniffing Dogs in the War on Terror

Since September 11, 2001, the federal government has recognized the special skills that trained dogs can bring to security efforts. Because of their strong sense of smell, dogs are able to detect explosives. The government, as well as many private organizations, has created training centers to teach people and dogs the necessary skills to work as K-9 teams. These centers are working to meet the demand for trained handlers and dogs to fight bomb threats.

The Department of Homeland Security maintains two major breeding and training centers for bomb-sniffing dogs. The centers teach canine teams—each made up of a dog and its handler—how to detect explosives and illegal drugs. They also teach people how to breed and train detection dogs. They offer ongoing instruction and retraining for handlers as well.

Dogs have an amazing sense of smell. Their noses are between one hundred and one thousand times more sensitive than humans'. Consider this: Humans can smell a hamburger. A dog can smell the meat, onion, pickles, ketchup, mustard, and bun. At bomb-sniffing schools, dogs are trained to locate anything that smells like an explosive.

"If you think the dog has found an odor but can't place exactly where it is, you have to know where to look. Your job is to get the dog to the most productive areas."

Inspector Melissa and her dog supported the Democratic and Republican national conventions and Secret Service operations. They did sweeps. This means they walked the dogs through an area before the public or officials arrived. Inspector Melissa has to know how her dog responds to his surroundings. In New Orleans after Hurricane Katrina hit, she patrolled the Joint Forces Operation Center for FEMA in Baton Rouge. She also did regular security checks at FEMA relief centers—tent and trailer compounds.

"If we're doing a sweep and the dog sits," Inspector Melissa says, "I report to the Explosive Ordinance Disposal (EOD) and get the dog out of the way. They send in the disposal team to neutralize the device or move it away to where it can be safely detonated. If you think the dog has found an odor but can't place exactly where it is, you have to know where to look. Your job is to get the dog to the most productive areas."

Inspector Melissa continues, "I've been almost three years with FPS and two years as a dog handler. I had no idea FPS had a handler position when I joined. Typically there are dogs assigned in major cities. Washington, D.C., has five dogs working, and there are not quite a hundred dogs on patrol in the United States."

In Chicago, inspector dog handler salaries start at $34,100 and top out at $60,500. Handlers get one hour of overtime a day for dog maintenance. The FPS provides the uniform, weapons, and equipment. Inspector Melissa carries a SIG Sauer P229 .357 semiautomatic pistol and has to requalify four times a year. She also has to recertify quarterly as a team with her dog.

An FPS officer wears a riot helmet while getting briefed for duty at the 2004 Republican National Convention.

"I really love it," Inspector Melissa says. She started her career in law enforcement in administration-management in the military police. She rose through the ranks to become a major in the army and a director of security. Her military service gave her law enforcement

"The difference with being an explosive dog handler is if you miss something, the possibility is there for real destruction and loss of life."

experience. Later, she worked as a director of campus security at the University of Colorado.

"Of all the schools and training programs I've done over the years, the K-9 training was the most difficult. You have to learn to do it well. The difference with being an explosive dog handler is if you miss something, the possibility is there for real destruction and loss of life. You have to be a well-trained team."

Inspector Melissa recommends that anyone interested in becoming a dog handler should arrange for a ride-along. He or she should accompany a handler on daily rounds for two or three days. She expects that most handlers would be open to providing an interested individual with some real-world experience. She says, "If someone came to me and asked to accompany me, I'd be okay with it."[7]

USSS and FPS agents must face difficult, often dangerous situations. They sometimes handle matters of life or death.

Antonio A. Cantu is the chief scientist for the Forensic Services Division of the USSS. He and his team examine evidence, such as fingerprints.

Support Jobs with the USSS and the FPS

Agents and officers on the front line of law enforcement cannot do their jobs without specially trained support personnel to keep their operations running smoothly. Many of these support personnel bring highly specialized skills to criminal investigation. They also take ordinary job skills and adapt them to the needs of their agency.

Support Jobs of the U.S. Secret Service

Like any law enforcement organization that faces criminal activity, the USSS must rely on the expertise of well-trained professionals. Some positions, such as fingerprint specialists and intelligence researchers, require specific training. Others involve running headquarters or offices. They are similar to the same positions with a company or a small business. The main ingredient that separates Secret Service support jobs from others is the secrecy required.

Before applicants are offered jobs, an in-depth check is made on their background—all the way back to childhood. Applicants must be U.S. citizens. They must pass a drug screen to prove that they do not use illegal substances. The agency contacts acquaintances, friends, and previous employers to ask questions about the applicant. School records are checked. The applicant must also pass a polygraph test, commonly called a lie-detector test.

All employees must qualify for top-secret security clearance. This means they go through a strict check to make sure that they can be trusted with secret information. Some jobs, such as data-entry or clerical positions, may not require direct contact with secret information. Still, every employee will come into contact with others who do have such information. Anything seen, heard, or read while working for the Secret Service must remain a secret forever.

The Secret Service employs hundreds of technical specialists. They work on projects dealing with criminal activity. This work requires knowledge from many sciences. Telecommunications and computer specialists help solve financial and computer crimes. Fingerprint and photographic specialists use the latest technology and digital imaging to investigate criminal activities. Secret Service specialists learn how to think like criminals while staying on the right side of the law.

Fingerprint Specialist

"When I came into the field of fingerprint identification, I immediately found it appealing," says a Secret Service fingerprint specialist. "My job is to analyze and catalog fingerprints, [which are] the most widely used method of identification for investigators. Today, everything is digitized, so finding comparisons can happen in a matter of minutes. Sometimes, however, the computer returns a few near-matches. And that's where my experience becomes valuable.

"I love this job for a lot of reasons," the specialist says. "It requires accurate analysis, speed, archival skills, and an investigative flair that relatively few people have. And I get to solve crimes. That's the most satisfying part."[1]

Some universities and colleges offer certificates and two- or four-year diplomas in forensic and crime scene investigation. Forensic science is used in courts of law to prove a case. Fingerprinting is the personal identification part of forensic investigation. Other branches include tool mark identification, forensic photography, and crime scene processing.

Digital Fingerprint Analysis

A fingerprint is an impression of the underside of the end of a finger or thumb. Fingerprints are used for identification because the pattern in any fingerprint is considered unique and permanent for every person. When a print is invisible, it must be made visible using brushed-on dust or other techniques. These invisible prints are called latent. This means they are present but not visible.

Fingerprints left at the scene of a crime are analyzed using the Universal Latent Workstation (ULW) at the Secret Service laboratory. Workers at the laboratory can scan the fingerprints or take a digital picture of them. The resulting image of a fingerprint is loaded into the ULW. It helps a fingerprint specialist encode the fingerprint, or scan it into digital information that a computer can use. This information is entered into a database. Law enforcement agencies can search this database.

The ULW is used to search latent fingerprints against the FBI's electronic fingerprint database or any local or state database across the country. Analysts can improve fingerprint images and then search for a matching print in the databases. At the Secret Service alone, the ULW has been responsible for more than a thousand suspect identifications.

Technical Positions

Technical employees at the USSS help agents and other professionals at the agency. Technical work involves knowledge gained through on-the-job experience or special training. Some technical staff ensure that only certain people have access to classified information. Photographers are also important to the USSS and serve various needs at the agency. They photograph crime scenes. They also use software to improve the quality of digital images so they provide more information for an investigation. Other specialists make sure that the equipment is operating well, analyze documents, search for fingerprints, and make sure agency buildings are secure.

Professional Positions

Professional positions at the USSS require scientific or other advanced knowledge. Usually this knowledge comes from a college education or specialized training. Professional employees provide advanced information, materials, and techniques to the Secret Service.

For example, it seems unlikely for an accountant to save the day. However, many criminals have been caught simply because they got their math wrong! It was not blazing machine guns that brought down Al Capone's criminal mob in Chicago in the 1930s. The crime buster was a federal accountant who noticed that Capone's bookkeeping was sloppy. Capone was locked up in a dank cell on Alcatraz Island for not paying his taxes.

Several types of professional jobs are available at the USSS. Some positions require advanced training. Opportunities are available in the following fields, to name just a few:

- accounting
- architecture
- law
- chemistry
- engineering (civil, electronics, and materials)
- nursing
- psychology

How would the Secret Service use the skills of a materials engineer? These professionals know how to develop machinery, tools, and techniques to meet the agency's needs. Materials engineers can also reverse-engineer an object. This means they take the object apart to see how it was made. Then they can determine what it was designed to do. Materials engineers might reverse-engineer anything from computer software to a timing device for a bomb.

Administrative Positions

"I could be a facilities management specialist for any number of companies," says a USSS specialist, "but not the way I do it for the Secret Service." Most facilities managers oversee a building. They make sure all the building systems, such as heat and electricity, were working properly. If they worked in a research building, they might take care of a special dust-free room.

"For the Secret Service, this is the most complex version of facilities management you can find. I take care of several facilities where security only *begins* with a lock on the door. There are fingerprint and DNA labs where critical evidence is discovered and kept. There are shooting ranges and special weapons storage—equipment that must stay out of the wrong hands. There are whole rooms filled with mainframe computers that have to be maintained at proper temperatures—special heating and cooling zones throughout the buildings."

The USSS specialist started out as a facilities manager for a computer manufacturer. There the biggest challenge was getting rid of dust. Everyone had to wear special suits, slippers on their shoes, and gloves. Even the smallest particles of dust could damage the circuit chips being constructed. The specialist also handled the manufacturer's complex air ventilation systems. According to the specialist, "The Secret Service has a few clean rooms too—in which they do very interesting things I can't talk about.

"This is the kind of ordinary job that becomes extraordinary in the Secret Service. I have a top-secret security clearance and am constantly exposed to sensitive information. I could do a similar job someplace else, but it wouldn't be anywhere near as interesting or challenging."[2]

Administrative positions involve using ideas and skills to run an organization. Many of these positions do not require education beyond high school. However, they do involve analysis, research, writing, and good judgment. Future USSS employees usually gain these skills through a general college education or through experience. The following list includes some of the administrative positions at the USSS:

- administrative officer
- criminal research specialist
- facilities management specialist
- intelligence research specialist
- management analyst
- personnel management specialist
- writer/editor

Forensic Services Division

Forensics is the use of scientific knowledge to solve crimes or to try a case in court. The Forensic Services Division (FSD) is one of the most important parts of the USSS. It brings together the work of many people to solve crimes. Forensic examiners in the FSD analyze documents, fingerprints, and false IDs or credit cards. They collect photographic, video, and audio evidence as well. Some examiners use special equipment or chemical analysis to look at evidence.

The FSD manages the Secret Service's polygraph program. It also runs the Voice Identification Program, which uses computer equipment to compare voice prints and to identify a speaker. The FSD even uses hypnosis to gather evidence about an event. Hypnosis can help a person remember the event better. The FSD

Polygraph: How Does It Work?

The human body reacts to stress and emotions in certain ways. For example, sweating might increase or the heart might beat faster. One type of stress that triggers these reactions is when a person tries to tell a lie. A polygraph—also called a lie detector—keeps track of these reactions. A polygraph is a device that measures blood pressure, heart rate, respiration (breathing rate), and skin conductivity (sweat or skin temperature). It compares these measurements to their normal levels.

Secret Service examiners conduct polygraph tests related to criminal or national security cases. They also test the agency's new employees, who will have access to top-secret information. Polygraphs do not actually detect lies. They only show that a person may be trying to hide something. Other things besides lying can cause similar body reactions. This is why an experienced examiner is an important part of a polygraph test. He or she is highly trained to tell the difference between anxiety and a possible case of deception.

has cutting-edge technology that is not found in any other law enforcement agency in the country. The following are just a few examples:

Handwriting Identification

The Forensic Information System for Handwriting (FISH) allows the Secret Service to create a database of handwriting samples. The system scans writing so it can be put on a computer. The computer then compares it with other writing samples in the database to see if there are matches. If a match is found, this evidence can be used in criminal cases.

Printed Document Identification

The Instrument Analysis Services Section of the USSS houses the International Ink Library. It is the most complete collection of inks worldwide, with more than seven thousand samples. This collection is used to identify the source of a writing sample. The collection helps an investigator find out the type of writing instrument that was used and the earliest possible date that a document could have been produced. The collection also includes samples of computer printer inks and toners.

Fingerprint Identification Services Section

The FSD also operates the Automated Fingerprint Identification System (AFIS). This network combines several fingerprint databases, including latent fingerprints collected through the Universal Latent Workstation.

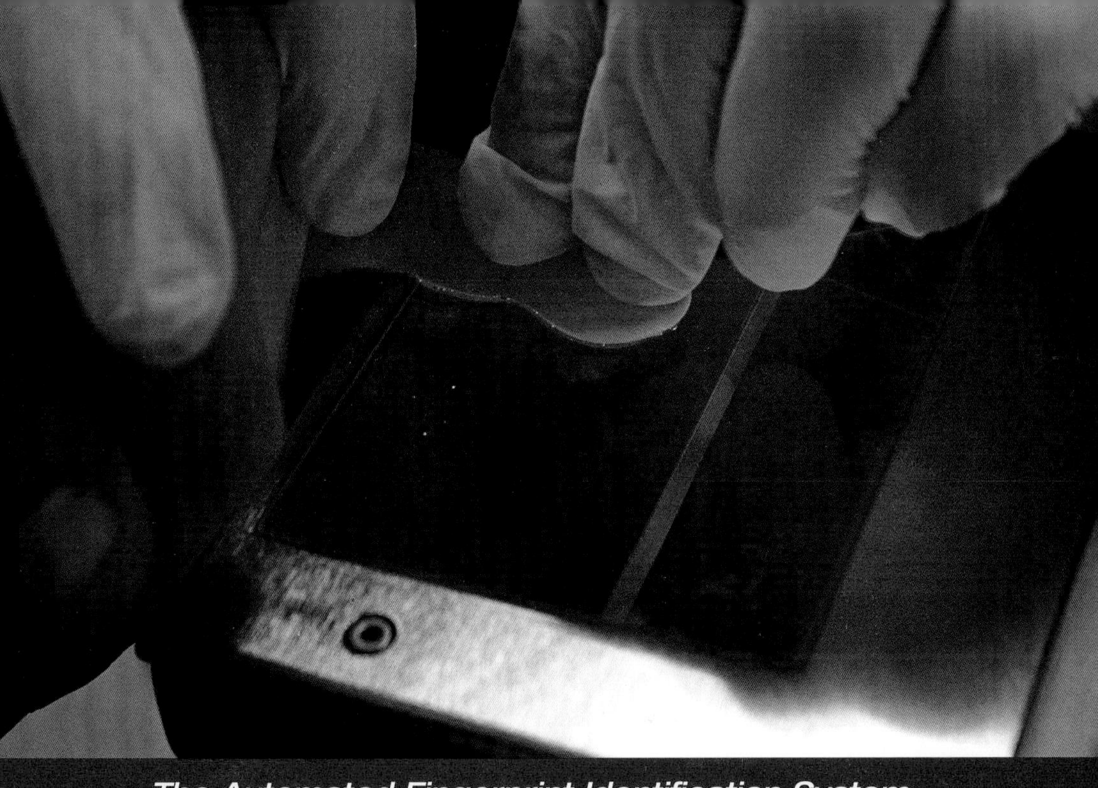

The Automated Fingerprint Identification System allows USSS employees to make digital recordings of millions of fingerprints.

It provides access to more than 30 million fingerprints. Using this system, a fingerprint specialist can digitize a fingerprint from an item of evidence and search for it in databases around the country. These findings often provide a suspect's name and other important information.

Polygraph Examination Program

The Polygraph Examination Program has improved the science of detecting deception. Polygraphs measure body functions such as breathing, pulse rate, and blood pressure. Polygraph examinations can help the Secret Service solve cases more quickly. This saves time and money.

Visual Information Services Section

The Visual Information Services Section provides photographic, graphic, and video services to the USSS. This work may include improving the quality of audio recordings or photographs to provide more information. Often, a blurred photograph or a small portion of a picture can be improved with computer technology. This gives investigators more information. The same can be done for audio recordings.

Support Jobs with the Federal Protective Service

The FPS has a large number of support employees. It uses employees of private firms for most of its clerical positions. These employees are hired and paid by companies that specialize in providing support people to government agencies or other organizations. Some support personnel do work directly for the FPS, however. The positions that follow are specially trained by the FPS.

FPS Contract Specialist

"I am an FPS contract specialist," Specialist Roger says. "That means I have a warrant to spend money. This warrant is like a hall pass or a permission slip to go to the library. It gives me permission to spend government funds to buy products and services for the FPS. There are five levels of warrants depending on the specialist's level of training and experience. I have an unlimited

FPS personnel talk with visitors about support positions during a law enforcement conference.

warrant, which is the highest level. With the highest level, I could buy a space shuttle for billions of dollars if the money was there to do it and the FPS needed one. Since neither of these events is likely, I deal with the day-to-day contracts needed to operate the agency.

"It's a lot of work, but it's necessary to keep all parts of FPS working well. Many FPS employees come from hiring firms outside the agency. These positions include secretarial and data-entry jobs, basic security guard services—any part of the work that doesn't require special FPS training and skills." One of Specialist Roger's jobs is to work with these firms to make sure FPS offices have the necessary staff.

What skills does a contract specialist need? According to Specialist Roger, "An applicant has to be well organized, logical, use careful record keeping, and be literate—he or she must know the meaning of words. Something can sound like one thing and mean something completely different. You have to be able to make yourself completely clear when you speak or put words down on paper or in a computer."

FPS contract specialists are business advisors for the federal government. They give advice to managers about goods and services they may need to purchase. Government contracts can be worth a lot of money. Take one recent contract to provide security guard services for about five years. The company that won the contract provides entry and exit guards for many FPS facilities. It will receive $100 million in payment for these services.

Contract specialists have to be both honest and knowledgeable. Even for simple purchases such as office supplies, specialists have to know how pricing works. Their job is to save the government money. Even so, the lowest bid for a contract may not always be the best. The company chosen for a contract must be honest and reliable, with a strong track record. Contract specialists have a lot of responsibility. The job requires training and experience.

"Starting out, contract specialists can expect $41,700 moving up to $60,500 base salaries."

"I've had about thirty courses in on-job training," Specialist Roger says. "Today, they are looking for people with master's degrees for this position—especially a master of business administration (MBA). They will take someone with bachelor's degree. If you want to learn, they will give you the experience.

"Starting out, contract specialists can expect $41,700 moving up to $60,500 base salaries. They begin with small warrants, making basic purchases, and learning the ropes. Gradually the warrants grow larger along with the responsibility for handling more money. Negotiation skills are a must for a contract specialist. As you create a new contract, you set it up to get a fair price for the contractor and a good deal for the government. If you make a mistake when awarding contracts in security and law enforcement, you're exposing somebody to risk or danger concerning their life or property."[3]

FPS Budget Supervisor

The FPS is a big organization. A large amount of money must be available for salaries, equipment, facilities, management, contracts, and training. Jobs in creating budgets for law enforcement have their own special qualifications.

"I've been with FPS for twenty-two years," says Budget Supervisor Alma. "It's my team of four individuals that has the responsibility to put together a budget and anticipate the needs of this FPS region. We do this every two years. We ask the folks in the field about their needs. They tell us the technology and staffing needs they see coming down the road. They give us information, and we come up with the amount of money needed to run this fiscal year. Once we get our budget back, we have to try and distribute the money fairly based on need and try to stay within that budget.

"The budget creation team has to have at least some idea of what each division does. They know about the basic needs—payroll for the officers and staff, vehicles, communications, all the way to the shoe allowance, which is a significant amount considering the thousands of miles

A Contract Specialist's Job During a Crisis

Sometimes contracts must be created quickly to cover emergency needs. Hurricane Katrina in 2005 was such an emergency. "At the New Orleans disaster," Specialist Roger says, "I rushed contracts and purchase orders through Washington. We set up Mobile Command Vehicles, each worth about $400,000. These are big trailers full of communications and computer equipment. They were vital to help check identities of people coming back to their homes—to make sure they really lived there. We provided the MCVs and their staff. We contracted satellite communications because all the radio and TV towers had been wrecked. Emergency supplies were trucked in to people in New Orleans—everything from life-saving medical supplies and electrical generators to insect repellent.

"We had to respond to requests from people on the scene. Some of our FPS officers and inspectors were still living in tents. Stores had been looted of basic supplies. FPS workers needed everything from toothpaste and razor blades to MREs [Meals-Ready to Eat] and bottled water. We even had to send out fresh FPS uniforms. After working the streets in that toxic mud and water for fourteen to sixteen hours a day, the cloth also became toxic and had to be burned."[4]

patrolled on foot every year. Anything over and above the norm, they ask—and hopefully they'll get it. Considering requests and allocations, we have to know where reality begins and fantasy ends," says Supervisor Alma.

"It helps that everyone in this group has fifteen years of service. I came on as a clerk typist, but that can't really happen today because all the secretarial positions are contracted out. I was working about a year when I heard that financial people were needed in the field, so I applied and spent four years in a district office. [Then] I applied for the regional office." Alma was hired at $34,000 per year and eventually began to work without supervision at $41,700. "When I first took this job, our total budget was $7 million. I thought that was too much money. Over time, budgets and workload grew.

"It's good to have an accounting or bookkeeping background—but they're totally different. Today, you really need a college degree to apply. We do data entry. The job requires computer skills and research abilities. We have special computer programs that are unique to the FPS agency.

"Applicants would come in at. . . $27,500 per year as a trainee. We offer a Trainee Program every year. Trainees are rotated to different positions so they learn about the agency. In regional and district field offices, a financial trainee will be interviewed by panels and recommended to the next higher grade until they reach journey [experienced] level: $50,500, $60,500, and above. This program was introduced to bring in college students. The FPS will work with their schedule, but they can only be in the program as long as they are full-time college students.

"My greatest satisfaction is enjoying the challenge, trying to keep us in the black [not spending more money than the agency has]. Also, this isn't our money—it belongs to the American people. I can't stress that enough. We question many things that are requested. The FPS is a great organization to work for."[5]

Security Specialist

"I came over as a secretary from a real estate job with the General Services Administration," says Specialist Doris. "I filled in with other jobs because they were short-handed. My full-time work as a security specialist started as an investigative aide back in 1992. At that time, the job was simpler. Decisions came from headquarters. I took classes in adjudication. This means acting like a judge—learning to look at evidence, arguments, and legal reasoning to decide if there is any reason to withhold a security clearance."

What is involved in a security clearance check? First, the person or company fills out an application. They answer questions about employment, personal history, and whether they have been arrested. The person also submits a fingerprint card. The FPS is most concerned about a person's criminal history. If the agency is doing a clearance check on a company, it

Before this FPS officer gained clearance to do high-security work, he had to go through a check with a security specialist.

checks to see if the company has been involved in any illegal activities.

"A security specialist needs good interviewing skills," says Specialist Doris. "Often we have to explain to employees and companies why we did not grant them a security clearance. You have to show documentation—all the paperwork that influenced your decisions. You're dealing with possible criminal information and people's ability to work. If they don't get that clearance, they can't work. We do hundreds of cases a month with deadlines to meet.

"Following the September 11, 2001, tragedy, we had to get clearances for emergency contracted guards completed in five days. We were issuing in half the time we usually need. We had to keep up with our regular work, too—people always work late around here to get the job done. Working nine to five never seems to happen."[6]

A security specialist starts out at $27,500 per year and can move up to $41,700 per year. To reach $34,100 per year, applicants need a two-year associate's college degree in any subject. At the entry level, they need experience in data entry, research, filing, and other basic clerical skills. Entry-level employees are not allowed to judge security clearance request cases until they get more experience. At the next level, a worker can adjudicate temporary clearances. Finally, after more experience, the specialist can make both temporary and final clearance adjudications.

A Secret Service member (left) talks with a woman about career opportunities in the agency.

Starting Your Career Path

Employment in the USSS and the FPS requires dedication to get the job. It also takes a lot of hard work to keep the job once you have it. Where is a good place to start? The USSS offers intern programs and suggested career paths for students. These are detailed in the remainder of this chapter. The FPS suggests contacting a local office to learn about student and intern programs.

The USSS Student Intern Program

The Student Intern Program provides unpaid work assignments. These jobs allow students to explore careers and to develop personal and professional skills. Students are expected to work at least twelve hours per week. They must work no less than one semester, two quarters, or a summer session.[1] All interns must be current students. The program offers many benefits[2]:

- career exploration beginning early in a student's academic work
- exposure to new and emerging occupations and technologies
- academic credit for the work performed (this is determined by the student's school)
- work experience that may be considered if the student later applies for permanent employment with the agency

The USSS Student Intern program is not intended to provide the intern with investigative or protective experience.

Students must meet the following requirements to be considered for an intern position[3]:

- be sixteen years of age
- be a U.S. citizen
- be enrolled or accepted for enrollment during the next semester or quarter as a full- or part-time student in high school or in an educational institution (not above the bachelor's level)
- have an agreement from the school to participate
- not be the son or daughter of a Secret Service employee
- complete a preliminary background investigation and drug screening

USSS student employment programs get people on the path to protecting U.S. leaders. These agents guard Secretary of State Condoleezza Rice and White House Chief of Staff Andrew Card.

The USSS Student Temporary Education Employee Program

This program helps students earn money and continue their education at the same time. Candidates for the Stay-in-School Program must meet financial guidelines through a state employment office or their school's financial aid office.[4] They can also be certified through the Secret Service Personnel Office.

Eligibility

Temporary Education Employee Program candidates must meet the following criteria[5]:

- be sixteen years of age at the time of their appointment
- be U.S. citizens
- be enrolled or accepted for enrollment during the upcoming semester or quarter as a full- or part-time student in high school or in an educational institution (not above the bachelor's level)
- be working toward a diploma, certificate, or degree
- maintain a satisfactory academic record of a 2.5 or better cumulative grade point average
- not be the son or daughter of a Secret Service employee

Assignment and Leave

Most of the program's assignments are of a clerical nature, and no previous experience is required. Students are eligible for paid annual and sick leave. For every twenty to twenty-four hours worked, one hour of sick leave and one hour of annual leave are given.[6]

Working Hours

Stay-in-school employees with the Secret Service work part-time while school is in session and full-time during summers and official school breaks.[7] While school is in session, students' work schedule is limited to a minimum of fifteen hours each week and a maximum of twenty-four hours a week. Working hours are determined by the office to which a student is assigned.

Salary and Promotions

The pay students receive depends on their education and work experience. As they advance in their education, they may be eligible for promotions based on work performance, grade point average, and credits earned.[8]

Eligibility and Verification for Continued Employment[9]

At the beginning of each fall semester or quarter, students are asked to produce a letter from their educational institution showing proof of enrollment for the upcoming semester or quarter. A copy of grades from the previous semester is required to show that the student still has a 2.5 or better grade point average. Students have two weeks from the beginning of the fall semester to submit verification.

Each year students are required to show proof of financial status to be eligible for the program. Unless they are granted a financial waiver from the USSS Personnel Office, they are required to produce a financial eligibility statement from the State Employment Office or a copy of a financial statement from their financial aid office. This is required once a year.

Conclusion

There are many employment opportunities available with the United States Secret Service and the Federal Protective Service. Preparation is the key with both agencies. Each agency has very high hiring standards and offers lifetime careers with full government benefits, including health care and a strong pension program. Law enforcement agencies have a need for a variety of skills ranging from police investigation to scientific analysis.

The Secret Service differs from the Federal Protective Service in the level of security clearance demanded at all levels. Even entry-level clerical personnel must be carefully screened at the USSS. The FPS, on the other hand, contracts out many of its entry-level jobs to professional hiring services. This includes security guard positions in places where fully trained FPS officers are not required. Most of their hiring begins with individuals who fit their skills to FPS needs. However, as described earlier, there are many high-level positions directly hired by the FPS.

There is a lot of information available about both agencies for anyone who wants to start a career in federal law enforcement. You, too, could protect the president of the United States, make sure critical supplies reach officers in dangerous locations, or insure the security of our government's offices. Full-time work in federal law enforcement offers job satisfaction and service to our country.

USSS and FPS Jobs at a Glance

USSS Positions

Special agent Uniformed Division officer	$29,000–$43,000 plus 25% availability pay
USSS supervisor	$72,000–$105,000

FPS Positions

Criminal investigator	Starts at $27,500
Uniformed officer	$27,500–$41,700
Budget supervisor	$27,000–$60,500
Dog handler	$34,100–$60,500
Contract specialist	$41,700–$60,500
Inspector	$47,000–$50,000
Uniformed lieutenant	$50,500
Uniformed captain	$60,500

Chapter Notes

Chapter 1. Two Agencies: Protecting Leaders and the People They Serve

1. Greg Simmons and the Associated Press, "Bush Visits Heart of New Orleans," *Fox News,* September 13, 2005, <http://www.foxnews.com/story/0,2933,169086,00.html> (July 11, 2006).

2. "ICE Law Enforcement Support Proves Critical to Hurricane Katrina Rescue and Security Efforts," *U.S. Immigration and Customs Enforcement,* September 8, 2005, <http://www.ice.gov/graphics/news/newsreleases/articles/050908washington.htm> (March 8, 2006).

3. Ibid.

Chapter 2. A Tale of Two Services

1. United States Secret Service Web site, n.d., <http://www.secretservice.gov/faq.shtml#training_sa> (March 8, 2006).

2. Ronald Reagan, "Reagan Quotes," *PBS: The American Experience,* n.d., <http://www.pbs.org/wgbh/amex/reagan/sfeature/quotes.html> (March 8, 2006).

3. "Timothy McCarthy," *University of Missouri, Kansas City: Famous Trials,* n.d., <http://www.law.umkc.edu/faculty/projects/ftrials/hinckley/mccarthy.htm> (March 8, 2006).

4. "Secret Service History—Timeline," *United States Secret Service,* n.d., <http://www.ustreas.gov/usss/history.shtml> (March 8, 2006).

5. "Historical Background—Federal Protective Service (FPS)" *U.S. Immigration and Customs Enforcement,* n.d., <http://www.ice.gov/graphics/fps/org_hb.htm> (March 8, 2006).

6. Senate Appropriations Committee, "Homeland Security: Actions Needed to Better Protect National Icons and Federal Office Buildings from Terrorism," *Government Accountability Office*, June 24, 2005, <http://www.gao.gov/htext/d05790.html> (March 8, 2006).

Chapter 3. Frontline Jobs with the United States Secret Service

1. Institute for Career Research, "Careers with the United States Secret Service, Institute Research Number 227," *Careers-internet.org*, n.d., <http://www.careers-internet.org> (March 8, 2006).

2. Ibid.

3. United States Secret Service Web Site, n.d., <http://www.secretservice.gov/faq.shtml#training_sa> (March 8, 2006).

4. Institute for Career Research, "Careers with the United States Secret Service, Institute Research Number 227," *Careers-internet.org*, n.d., <http://www.careers-internet.org> (March 8, 2006).

5. Ibid.

Chapter 4. Frontline Jobs with the Federal Protective Service

1. Interview with FPS Special Agent Cleo, Kluczynski Federal Building, 230 South Dearborn Street, Chicago, Ill., October 19, 2005.

2. Ibid.

3. "Infant's Life Saved by Federal Protective Service Guard," *U.S. Immigration and Customs Enforcement*, August 26, 2004, <http://www.ice.gov/pi/news/newsreleases/articles/082604fps guard.htm> (August 7, 2006).

4. Ibid.

5. Interview with FPS Uniformed Officer George, Kluczynski Federal Building, 230 South Dearborn Street, Chicago, Ill., October 19, 2005.

6. Interview with FPS Inspector Elizabeth, Kluczynski Federal Building, 230 South Dearborn Street, Chicago, Ill., October 19, 2005.

7. Interview with Inspector/K-9 Dog Handler Melissa, by telephone to New Orleans duty station, October 15, 2005.

Chapter 5. Support Jobs with the USSS and the FPS

1. Institute for Career Research, "Careers with the United States Secret Service, Institute Research Number 227," *Careers-internet.org*, n.d., <http://www.careers-internet.org> (March 8, 2006).

2. Ibid.

3. Interview with FPS Contract Specialist Roger, by telephone, Kluczynski Federal Building, 230 South Dearborn Street, Chicago, Ill., October 24, 2005.

4. Ibid.

5. Interview with FPS Budget Supervisor Alma, by telephone, Kluczynski Federal Building, 230 South Dearborn Street, Chicago, Ill., October 24, 2005.

6. Interview with FPS Security Specialist Doris, by telephone, Kluczynski Federal Building, 230 South Dearborn Street, Chicago, Ill., October 24, 2005.

Chapter 6. Starting Your Career Path

1. "Employment Opportunities: Student Volunteer Service (Internship)," *United States Secret Service*, n.d., <http://www.secretservice.gov/opportunities_interns.shtml> (September 5, 2006).

2. Ibid.

3. Ibid.

4. "Employment Opportunities: Stay-In-School Program," *United States Secret Service*, n.d., <http://www.secretservice.gov/opportunities_stay-in-school.shtml> (September 5, 2006).

4. Ibid.

5. Ibid.

6. Ibid.

7. Ibid.

8. Ibid.

9. Ibid.

assassination—The killing of an important public figure.

assault—Used for the purpose of a military attack.

cardiopulmonary resuscitation (CPR)—A technique used to revive victims of a cardiac arrest (meaning that the heart has stopped).

clearance—Permission to work with confidential government materials or to enter a building where such work occurs.

closed-circuit television—Television that is shown to a limited number of viewers, such as security personnel.

confidential—Private or secret.

counterfeiting—Copying something, such as money, from an original and passing it off as real.

counterterrorism—Against people who use force or violence to try to overthrow a government or to disrupt a society.

covert—Secret.

cyber crime—Crime that is committed using technology, especially computers.

deserted—Emptied of people.

detonated—Set off; caused to explode.

diabetes—A disorder that causes extreme thirst and the production of large amounts of urine.

drug screen—Tests that examine urine or blood samples for traces of illegal substances.

exposed—Out in the open.

federal—Having to do with the national government of the United States, rather than state or local governments.

felony—A serious federal crime, such as murder or robbery, that is punishable by a long prison sentence.

fiscal year—The twelve-month period that businesses use for accounting purposes.

forensic—Relating to the use of knowledge or technology to prepare evidence for a court case or to solve a legal problem.

forgery—The crime of creating a fake document, such as a check.

fraud—Illegal deception or cheating for personal gain.

humanitarian—Promoting the health and general welfare of people.

identity theft—The crime of stealing another person's identity by using confidential information about them, such as a Social Security number or credit card numbers.

inauguration—Ceremony celebrating a leader who is entering office.

inconspicuous—Not easily noticeable.

intelligence—Information that concerns an enemy, a possible enemy, or an area.

interrogation—Questioning someone, especially a suspect in a crime, to find out information.

labor unions—Groups of workers who organize to make sure they are treated fairly.

looting—Stealing, especially in times of war or disaster.

money laundering—Concealing the ownership and source of stolen money by sending it through a legitimate source.

motorcade—A long line of cars.

mouth-to-mouth resuscitation—A technique in which a person helps another person breathe.

neutralize—To counteract the effect of something, such as a bomb.

personnel—Employees.

precautions—Acts that prevent harm; safeguards.

smugglers—People who try to bring goods or people into a country illegally.

surveillance—A watch kept over a person or place.

SWAT (Special Weapons and Tactics) team—A group of law enforcement officials who are highly trained in the use of special weapons and stopping criminals.

trafficking—Trading or selling something, such as illegal drugs.

transactions—Exchanges of goods or money.

vandalizing—Damaging property.

ventilation—Involving the circulation of air.

Books

Beyer, Mark. *Secret Service.* New York: Children's Press, 2003.

Gaines, Ann Graham. *The U.S. Secret Service.* New York: Chelsea House, 2001.

Owen, David. *Police Lab: How Forensic Science Tracks Down and Convicts Criminals.* Tonawanda, N.Y.: Firefly Books, 2002.

Seidman, David. *Secret Service Agents: Life Protecting the President.* New York: Rosen Publishing Group, 2003.

Internet Addresses

Federal Protective Service

<http://www.ice.gov/about/fps/contact.htm>

Secret Service

<http://www.secretservice.gov>

Federal Government Jobs

<http://www.usajobs.com>

FEDERAL PROTECTIVE SERVICE